# Kids Can Do It!

# I CAN BUILD A FORT!

by Ruth Owen

WINDMILL
BOOKS ™

Published in 2018 by **Windmill Books,** an Imprint of Rosen Publishing
29 East 21st Street, New York, NY 10010

Produced for Rosen by Ruby Tuesday Books Ltd
Designer: Tammy West

Photo Credits: Courtesy of Ruby Tuesday Books and Shutterstock.

Cataloging-in-Publication Data
Names: Owen, Ruth.
Title: I can build a fort! / Ruth Owen.
Description: New York : Windmill Books, 2018. | Series: Kids can do it! | Includes index.
Identifiers: ISBN 9781499483505 (pbk.) | ISBN 9781499483444 (library bound) |
    ISBN 9781499483833 (6 pack)
Subjects: LCSH: Fortification—Design and construction—Juvenile literature. |
    Children's playhouses—Design and construction—Juvenile literature.
Classification: LCC TH4967.O94 2018 | DDC 530.8—dc23

Manufactured in the United States of America
CPSIA Compliance Information: Batch BS17WM: For Further Information contact Rosen Publishing, New York, New York at 1-800-237-9932

# WARNING:

Some of the activities in this book require adult help.
It's also important that all laws and regulations are followed when carrying
out the activities in this book. The author and publisher disclaim any liability
in connection with the use of the information in this book.

# CONTENTS

# IT'S TIME FOR AN ADVENTURE!

Do you ever dream of having a hideaway or a secret place to hang out with your friends? Maybe you'd like a space that's all your own — with no adults allowed. If so, it could be time to build a fort!

You can build a fort in a forest, park, or backyard. You can even build one in your bedroom. Fort building is something you can do on your own or with friends.

You don't need lots of money to build a fort — just a little **creativity** and lots of imagination. So get dreaming and building, and let the adventure begin!

A garden shed fort

A forest fort

# USE YOUR IMAGINATION

Building a fort requires you to become a **designer**, a builder, and a problem solver.

This cozy indoor fort was made by draping sheets over a table.

This forest hideaway is made from branches and chunks of bark stacked against a tree trunk.

With a little imagination, even cardboard boxes can become a cool fort (see page 22).

# SAFETY TIPS FOR BUILDING FORTS

Building a fort should be a great adventure, so make sure it stays fun by following some important safety tips.

Only build a fort in a place where you have permission to play and build.

Build your fort in a safe place. Avoid building close to rivers or ponds. Don't build near old, dead trees or under dead, hanging branches.

Don't damage trees by snapping off live branches. Only use branches and leaves that have already fallen from trees.

Build carefully! You don't want the fort to collapse on you.

Do not disturb wild animals or their nests.

This fort was made from wood and junk that washed up on a beach.

Be respectful of other people who are spending time in places such as parks, forests, and beaches.

Never leave behind trash when building a fort outdoors.

When building outdoors, wear tough boots or shoes, and wear gloves to protect your hands from thorns and insects.

Always make sure an adult knows where you will be and what you will be doing. Carry a cell phone and call or text home regularly.

# A FOREST FORT

If you're able to spend the day in a forest, it's the perfect place to build a fort.

In a forest you might find natural, fort-like hiding places.
Old fallen tree trunks create natural places to find shelter.

The twisted, tangled roots of a fallen tree can become a secret hideaway. Always make sure your natural fort is secure!

In a forest you can find branches, ferns, and dead leaves for building.

Other visitors to the forest might use your fort. They may even take away parts of your structure to build a fort of their own!

A forest fort that's built only from natural materials can be left in place once you go home.

## When building forts in a forest, carry some basic equipment:

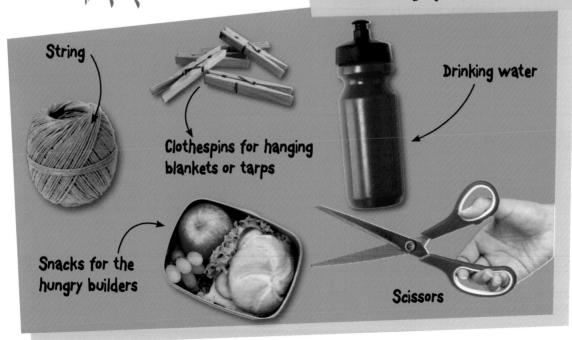

String

Clothespins for hanging blankets or tarps

Drinking water

Snacks for the hungry builders

Scissors

# BUILD A TEPEE

A forest is the perfect location to build a tepee-inspired fort. You'll need branches, leaves, string, and scissors or a pocket knife.

**1** Gather as many long, thick branches as you can. Branches that are about 6 feet (2 m) long will be best.

**2** Lay the branches on the ground in a neat bundle. Tightly tie the branches together with string close to one end.

**3** Stand up the bundle of branches with the tied end at the top. Carefully pull the bottom of each branch outward to make an evenly-spaced tepee shape.

**4** To make the tepee framework thicker, lay more branches against the tepee shape. Position these branches so the end of each branch slots in to the top point of the tepee.

**5** Make a covering for the tepee by gathering fern **fronds**, dead plant stems, and shorter, leafy branches.

Weave these materials between the upright branches.

This fort design is inspired by Plains Indians' tepees. Many Native American groups in the Great Plains region lived in tepees made of wooden poles and buffalo skins.

Search for logs or flat rocks to use as seats inside your fort.

# A FOREST LEAN-TO FORT

This lean-to fort can be built in a forest or woodland where there are lots of young trees with thin trunks.

**1** Find two thin trees that are growing about 6 feet (2 m) apart.

Crossbeam

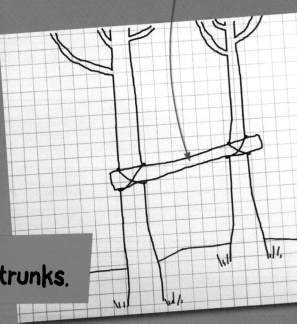

**2** To make a crossbeam, find a thick branch that will reach from one tree to the other.

Tie the branch tightly to the tree trunks.

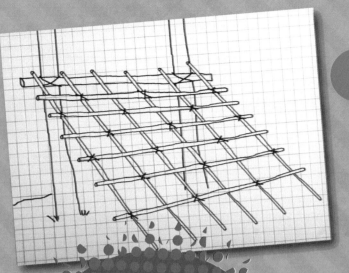

**3** Gather about 12 branches that are 6 feet (2 m) long. Lay six of the branches against the crossbeam.

Then lay the other six branches across the upright branches to make a crisscross grid. Tie the branches together where two branches cross over each other.

You don't have to tie the branches at every crossing point. Just tie as many as you need to make the grid sturdy and secure.

Moss

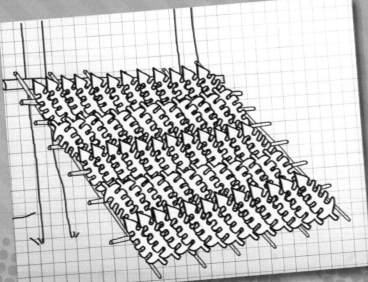

**4** Finally, cover the grid of branches with ferns, large leaves, and lumps of **moss**. Only use dead or fallen plants that you can identify.

A finished lean-to fort

**5** To make a floor for the fort, you can clear the ground back to bare dirt. Alternatively, you can place a plastic sheet or tarp inside the fort.

If you can't find two trees to use as the starting point for your fort, you can make the grid and lean it against a bank or the trunk of a large fallen tree.

You can also collect dry leaves and moss to make a soft, natural floor covering.

# MAKE FOREST STRING

It makes sense to carry string if you're fort building. However, it's also possible to make your own natural bindings from materials available in a forest.

Wild honeysuckle and ivy are trailing plants with soft but tough stems. You'll often find these plants spreading over the ground or climbing over trees. Use scissors to snip off a section to use as string. Cutting some of these plants won't harm them.

Ivy growing on a tree

Honeysuckle stem

Many plants have stems that can be split into strands that are soft but tough. These strands can be braided together to make rope.

Braided rope made from plant stems

# A WILDLIFE WATCHING FORT

If you love to watch birds or spot wild animals, try building a fort for wildlife watching.

This type of fort is often called a **blind**. It is a **camouflaged** shelter that can be used for quietly watching wild animals without them seeing you.

**1** Find a quiet spot among trees or bushes where you will have lots of chances to see birds and other animals.

**2** Before building the fort, make sure the ground is not too hard or rocky. You may be sitting or laying in your hide for long periods of time, so you will need to be comfortable.

**3** Find a thick, straight branch that's about 6 feet (2 m) long. This will be the fort's ridgepole.

A tripod

Ridgepole

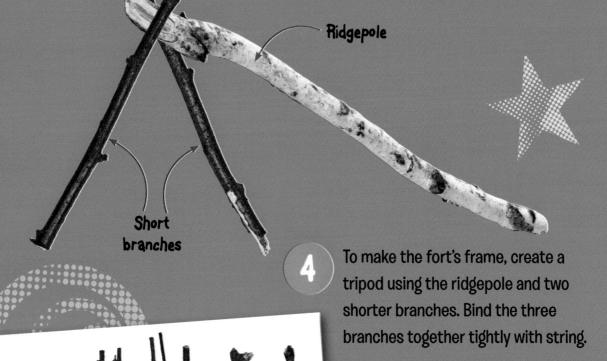

Short branches

**4** To make the fort's frame, create a tripod using the ridgepole and two shorter branches. Bind the three branches together tightly with string.

**5** Next, collect about 60 to 70 sticks of different lengths.

Ridgepole

Sticks of different lengths

**6** Prop the sticks along both sides of the ridgepole, like ribs. The fort's frame is now complete.

Bark

Fern frond

Moss

Pine tree branches

**7** Now gather materials to cover the frame. You can use leafy branches, pine tree branches, fern fronds, pieces of bark, and moss.

Cover the framework with a thick layer of these materials.

**8** Cover the ground inside the fort with ferns and leaves, too.

Does your hide blend in with the surrounding environment? To test this, walk away a short distance and then look back. Does it stand out from the surrounding plants, or is it well camouflaged?

**9** Climb inside the blind with your wildlife-watching equipment, get comfortable, and then stay still and quiet.

Notebook and pen

Camcorder

Binoculars

# A TOOLSHED FORT

If there's an old toolshed in your backyard that no one uses, ask if you can adopt it and turn it into a fort.

Maybe a friend or relative has an old summerhouse or shed that can become a place for you and your friends to hang out.

## IT'S ALL ABOUT TEAMWORK

Before you move into your new fort, ask an adult to check that the building is safe and sturdy.

1 Get together a clean-up team to sweep and tidy the shed.

2 Get permission to paint the fort. Ask the adults you know if they have any leftover paint from decorating projects that you can use.

Try mixing bright colors and personalizing your fort with handprints and other patterns.

**3** Find out if there are any pieces of unwanted furniture in attics or basements that you can have for your fort. Visit **yard sales**, too, and you might be able to buy chairs or small dressers for just a few dollars.

Put down colorful rugs on the floor.

Give your fort a name. You can also have a secret password that all visitors must say before they're allowed inside!

**4** You can hang up strings of battery-powered, colored lights. And pin up your favorite pictures on the walls.

What will you do in your toolshed fort? That's up to you! Why not listen to music or play games? It can be a place to keep things that are special to you. Maybe you can even have a sleepover with friends!

# CARDBOARD BOX MAZE FORT

This fantastic fort can be built indoors if you have enough space. If not, it's a perfect project for a backyard or playground.

To build a cardboard box **maze** fort you will need to do some advance preparation.

You will need to collect cardboard boxes that are big enough for you and your friends to crawl through. The kinds of boxes that hold appliances, such as washing machines, are just right. Tough boxes that people use for moving will also be great.

# YOU WILL NEED:

Tell everyone you know that you're collecting cardboard boxes. You can store them flattened until you're ready to start building.

Your boxes can all be the same size, or a mixture of shapes and sizes.

To make the fort, you will also need some other basic equipment.

**Duct tape or packing tape**

**Strings of white or colored battery-powered lights**

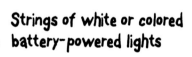

**Scissors or a craft knife**

## IT'S ALL ABOUT TEAMWORK

When you're using a craft knife or scissors, always make sure an adult is close by. You can also ask the adult to help you. But remember, no adults allowed inside the finished fort!

## Once you're ready to build your fort, think about what shape you'd like to create.

This maze has 11 large boxes.

Open corner

Closed end

Open end

Open end

Tower

Closed end

Here are some ideas for other maze shapes you could create from boxes.

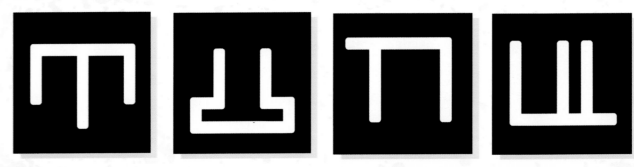

**1** Start by slotting together two cardboard boxes. Tuck the flaps of one box inside the other. You can then use tape to hold the boxes together.

**2** Attach a third box, leaving the corner open as an entrance.

**3** You can add a lookout tower at one corner.

**4** Some of these boxes are closed on one side. They can be "rooms" or dead ends in the maze. Other sections are open, so the fort has more than one entrance and exit.

**5** Using a craft knife, you can carefully cut an escape hatch in the top of one section.

**6** If you're going to spend time in your fort at night, you can add lights to some of the sections. Take the first bulb on a string of battery-powered lights. Pierce a hole in the top of one section of the fort and push the bulb through the hole.

Holes for lightbulbs

Battery-powered lights

Keep piercing holes for each of the bulbs on the string.

When darkness falls, switch on your lights and crawl into the illuminated tunnels of your maze fort.

**7** Make your maze fort comfortable inside with blankets, rugs, and cushions.

**8** When you get tired of the fort, you can take it apart and rebuild it in a different shape!

# AN INDOOR TENT FORT

If you don't have an outside space, or at times of the year when it's too cold or dark to be outdoors, build a fort inside!

All you need to build an indoor tent fort is some chairs and sheets or curtains.

**1** Begin by setting out six chairs. The seats of the chairs should be facing toward the outside.

**2** Drape sheets, curtains, or thin blankets over the chairs to create a tent.

**3** Place rugs, quilts, and cushions inside the fort to make it comfortable.

**4** Add some sparkle with strings of battery-powered lights and LED candles.

Climb inside and you've got your own cozy space for chatting with friends, reading, or just chilling out.

**blind**
A small, camouflaged shelter used for watching wildlife.

**camouflaged**
Blending in with the surroundings. A person, animal, or object can be hidden by using camouflage.

**creativity**
The use of imagination and new ideas to create something.

**designer**
A person who plans and creates the look of something, or how it will work.

**fronds**
The leaflike parts of plants such as ferns and palm trees.

**maze**
A network of paths, hedges, or corridors designed as a puzzle that a person has to find a way through. A maze has openings and dead ends.

**moss**
Tiny plants that grow close together, forming a green carpet-like covering on rocks or trees.

**yard sales**
Events organized in yards or driveways where people sell off secondhand items they no longer need at low prices.

## WEBSITES

For web resources related to the subject of this book, go to:
**www.windmillbooks.com/weblinks** and select this book's title.

# INDEX